THE DRUG WAR

First published in 1990
in the United States by
Gloucester Press
387 Park Avenue South
New York NY 10016

Design: Rob Hillier, Andy Wilkinson
Editor: Jen Green
Picture researcher: Cecilia Weston-Baker
Illustrator: Trev Lawrence

Printed in Belgium

Library of Congress Cataloging-in-Publication Data

Parker, Steve.
    The drug war / Steve Parker
        p. cm. -- (Issues)
    Summary: Discusses various aspects of the war against drugs, including the debate whether the focus should be on controlling domestic users and sellers or on fighting foreign drug barons.
    ISBN 0-531-17241-4
    1. Drug abuse--United States--Juvenile literature. 2. Drug abuse and crime--United States--Juvenile literature. 3. Drug abuse--United States--Prevention--Juvenile literature. 4. Drug traffic--United States--Juvenile literature. [1. Drug abuse and Crime. 2. Drug traffic.] I. Title.
HV5825.P27 1990
363.4'5'0973--dc20   90-3213   CIP   AC

The author, Steve Parker, is a writer and editor in the life sciences, health and medicine. He has edited 12 titles in the *Understanding Drugs* series for Aladdin Books and worked for 18 months on a medical weekly journal.
The consultant, Dr. Cindy Fazey, is a research fellow at the Centre for Urban Studies at the University of Liverpool. She has acted as consultant on drugs for both UNESCO and the United Nations.

Contents

THE DRUG WAR

STEVE PARKER

Gloucester Press

New York : London : Toronto : Sydney

World War Three?

"The greatest menace of our time" ... "the most serious threat to civilized society" ... "the next world war."

The threat is drugs. Illegal drugs, such as heroin, cocaine, amphetamines, LSD, and marijuana. The past few decades have seen an explosion of illegal drug use, especially in affluent Western countries. To meet the demand, production has mushroomed in poorer countries in the Middle East, southwest and southeast Asia, and South America.

There are an estimated 120,000 drug addicts in Britain; some five million Americans use cocaine. Numbers rise monthly, and almost every major city has its drug quarter.

▷ Antinarcotics forces raid a small cocaine processing laboratory. Dozens of such raids each year are part of the cleanup operation deep in the Colombian jungle.

Drugs bring many risks. Permanent ill health, job loss, the breakup of families and relationships, addiction, diseases like hepatitis and AIDS, overdose, death. And where drugs go, crime follows. War has been declared on illegal drugs. It is a real war, involving the armed forces, spies and undercover agents. It is being fought on many fronts: against drug growers, manufacturers, drug lords and organized crime syndicates, couriers and smugglers, wholesalers and street dealers, and drug users.

The drug trade – wealthy, powerful and well-armed – is fighting back. The drug war is "the war we cannot afford to lose."

Fueling a need

At either end of the drug business, the growers and users of drugs know little of each other. The peasant farmers in the poor countries of Asia and South America, where most drug producing plants are grown, know only that someone will pay for what they grow. They receive more income from drug crops than for food crops or commodity crops such as cocoa or cotton. Their needs consist of making a living for themselves and their families.

Drug plants are in some ways ideal crops. Opium poppies for heroin grow on difficult terrain, with no fertilizer and little water. Their value is high: $450 per year in some areas for an average family plot. Coca leaves used for cocaine can be harvested up to six times per year, and the plants thrive and go on producing leaves for 30 years. The economies of whole countries would be ruined without the drug exports.

▽ President George Bush declared "war on illegal drugs" as one of his top priorities after coming to office in 1989.

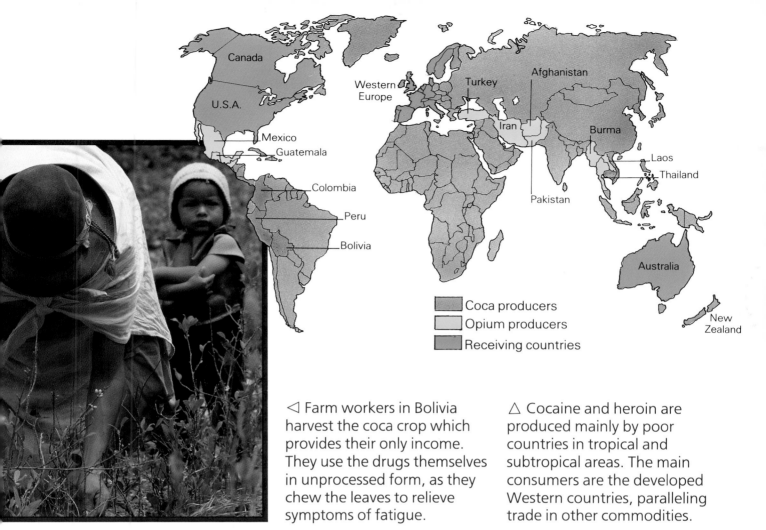

Canada

Western Europe

Turkey

Afghanistan

U.S.A.

Iran

Burma

Mexico

Guatemala

Laos

Thailand

Colombia

Pakistan

Peru

Bolivia

Australia

New Zealand

■ Coca producers
■ Opium producers
■ Receiving countries

◁ Farm workers in Bolivia harvest the coca crop which provides their only income. They use the drugs themselves in unprocessed form, as they chew the leaves to relieve symptoms of fatigue.

△ Cocaine and heroin are produced mainly by poor countries in tropical and subtropical areas. The main consumers are the developed Western countries, paralleling trade in other commodities.

In Peru the illegal trade in cocaine is estimated at $1,500 million per year – equivalent to half the annual legal exports. Similarly, the economy of Bolivia would probably collapse without income from cocaine exports.

At the other end of the chain are the users. Many factors combine to produce a need for the escapism that drugs provide in the West: shortage of jobs; low morale; the present uncertain trends in world economies; bigotry and discrimination; poor housing conditions; lack of educational opportunities. In Britain in 1989 the number of heroin addicts increased 17 percent over the previous year to 15,000. Cocaine seizures were 100 kilos higher, at 400 kilos. In the United States, the weights of illegal drugs seized in 1988, compared with the previous year, were 29 percent up for cocaine (to 198,000 pounds), and 35 percent up for heroin (to 2,150 pounds).

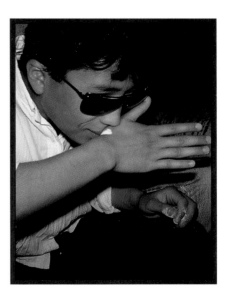

△ In the 1960s, cocaine was an expensive drug used mainly by the rich and famous. New processing and marketing methods have made it much cheaper.

◁ Fairy-tale castle owned by a Colombian drug trafficker in Chia. Inset: luxury bathroom of Rodríguez Gacha, of the Medellín cartel in Colombia.

Private armies

Thousands of peasant farmers and addicts form the wide base of the drug empire's pyramid. At the top are the few rich, powerful and ruthless drug lords.

In Colombia, the two cities of Medellín and Cali each have drug cartels. Members of these cartels are believed to be among the richest people in the world. Their business is outside the law and tax system, so they pay no taxes on their wealth. These drug lords are immensely powerful people. Some of them live respectable lives, send their children to expensive European schools, and have friends in high places in the government, judiciary and armed forces.

The wealth of the drug lords is vast. In Colombia, their trade is worth $5,000 million per year. They command their empires by fear, extortion, intimidation, bribery, violence, and murder. They surround and protect themselves with a network of people who take their risks.

Changing masters
Peasant farmers north-east of Laos grow opium poppies. Their crops were "encouraged" by the French, then by the Americans (to support addicted troops from Korea and Vietnam), and now by the militia of arch opium trader, General Vang Pau. An ex-CIA mercenary now commanding an army of Hmong tribesmen, his name intimidates the villagers. They live with guerrilla warfare as his soldiers protect the opium crop from troops and bandits, with heavy shelling and Mig-21 fighter jets.

The drug lords enforce their orders with their own private armies, fully armed and driven by both fear and greed for money. Mutiny in the army ranks is punishable by death, or by being handed over to the drug enforcement authorities. Luis Garcia, who ferried drugs from Colombia to Miami, turned his people over to the Drug Enforcement Administration (DEA) when they asked for higher wages.

The private armies of the drug lords guard the drug production and distribution chain, from the fields to the smuggling routes, against both government antidrug troops and rival drug gangs. They intimidate the farmers if they give up growing the crops. In Peru in 1985, 40 coca plantation workers were massacred because they refused to work. The laboratories where the drugs are processed, the airfields where they are flown from, and the luxury homes of the drug lords themselves are all heavily guarded.

△ Deadly business: a small arsenal of pistols, automatic weapons and ammunition found hidden in the home of a South American cocaine trafficker, in 1989.

Drugs finance guns
The private armies of the drug lords are fully armed with the most modern weapons. Drug enforcement agents capture more weapons each year. But there seems no limit to the source of these guns. In fact, illegal drug profits themselves finance another deadly and unlawful trade, in illegal arms shipments.

Pocket politicians

The drug lords are supported by international organized crime syndicates such as the Mafia. The Triad Gangs defend the opium trade in southeast Asia, while the Yardies from Jamaica support the cocaine trade in the United States and Britain. In Peru, the main drug protection comes from the *Sendero Luminoso*, or Shining Path, terrorist group. There are links between these gangs and terrorist organizations in other parts of the world.

Using their currencies of wealth and intimidation, the drug lords have woven protective networks around themselves, involving politicians and judges. The drug trade depends on a certain level of corruption in the government, to keep the trade routes open and to maintain the illegality of drugs. Far higher profits come from illegal drugs than from legal businesses. Occasionally the corrupt officials allow a drug seizure, for publicity purposes.

Revolution!
General García Meza (see opposite), financed by the drug lords, overthrew the Bolivian government in 1980. The army prevented the elected president, Hernan Siles Zuazo, from taking office until 1982. Since independence from Spain in 1825, Bolivia has had almost 200 civil and military uprisings.

▽ The shooting of Paul Castellano, Mafia leader, in New York in 1986. The Mafia became involved in drugs as an extension of its illegal supply of alcohol during the Prohibition era. In Washington in 1989, there were almost two murders daily — two thirds were drug-linked.

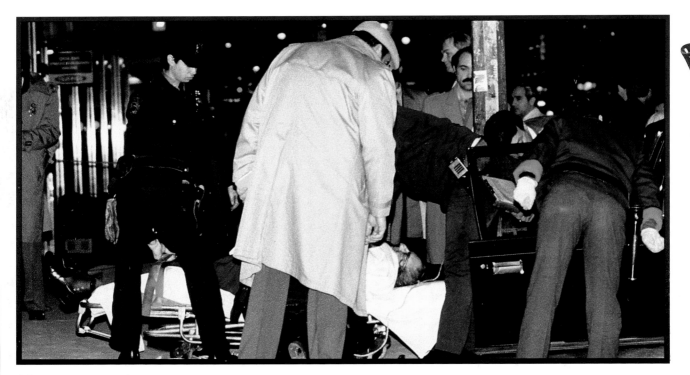

Corruption occurs in governments at all levels. The Colombian Ministry of Defense managed to "lose" a consignment of bulletproof vests, imported to protect judges engaged in the war against drugs.

In Colombia in 1984, President Betancur stepped up the war against cocaine. But Betancur's press office was believed to be the source of cocaine smuggled by diplomats to Spain, and thence to Europe.

In 1985, a Drug Enforcement Administration agent, Enrique Camarena Salazar, was murdered after apparently uncovering the corruption of many officials in the Mexican administration. Nineteen Mexicans have been indicted in Los Angeles, including two high level (former) police officers. In 1989, a member of the Liberal party of Colombia, Ivan Marulandra, suggested that up to 40 percent of Colombia's congressmen have been elected, knowingly or otherwise, with drug money.

△ General García Meza

▽ In 1982, Thai government troops attacked the headquarters of drug lord Khun Sa (below). About 80 of his men died, but the drug warlord escaped.

Extradition and confiscation

When narcotics authorities unravel a drug chain, and find the names of people at or near the top, two of the weapons that can be used against the traffickers are extradition and confiscation. Extradition is the surrender of an alleged criminal by one country to another, for trial. Many extradition treaties – agreements between countries that this may take place – have been signed between the drug-producing and Western nations, so that warrants for the arrest of known drug traffickers can be effective even over international borders.

The drug cartels respond to the threat of extradition with violence. In 1983, the President of Colombia approved the extradition of several drug traders to the United States. This resulted in the bombing of the American embassy and death threats to the American ambassador.

△ General Noriega of Panama was apprehended by US forces in January 1990.

"Los Extraditables"
Narcotics authorities on the trail of traffickers can issue warrants for their arrest that cross international borders. The leaders of Colombian drug cartels are wanted for trafficking. They are known as "Los Extraditables" because the Colombian government is trying to flush them out of hiding and extradite them to the United States for trial.

△ Medellín drug lord Jose Gonzalo Rodríguez Gacha attempted to deposit over $6.5 million in a Swiss bank. Officials became suspicious about the source of the money. The transaction was blocked by a Zurich court because he is wanted in the United States.

△ General Manuel Noriega, the dictator of Panama, was a powerful drug trafficker. His army, the National Defense Force, prevented democratic elections until 1989. The United States offered to assist the people of Panama in their fight for free elections. President Guillermo Endara won the election, but Noriega overturned its ruling, and had Endara publicly beaten up. United States forces stepped in to arrest Noriega. He sought refuge in the Vatican Mission in Panama, but surrendered eventually after the Mission advised him to leave.

In 1985 the Colombian Supreme Court suspended extradition of drug traffickers to the United States, in return for a promise by the cartels that they would abandon their trade. The drug lords did not honor the agreement.

Drugs seized by drug enforcement officers and profits from the drug trade can be confiscated by the state. However, the money made from drug dealing is difficult to trace. It is "laundered," or disguised, by passing it through corrupt or unknowing financial institutions. In Britain, since the Drug Trafficking Offenses Act was passed in 1986, banks have been required to notify police of suspicious deposits of large sums of money. Between January 1987 and May 1989, British courts filed confiscation orders totalling $20 million. Even so, in Britain alone it is estimated that drug tradings top $5 billion.

The military option

A major strategy in the drug war is to destroy the fields where the drug crops grow, the laboratories where they are processed, and the airstrips used to ferry out the prepared drugs. Armies and air forces bomb airstrips and set fire to laboratories. They even spray defoliants such as paraquat on the fields, to kill the growing plants and expose hideaway laboratories.

Poppies, coca or cannabis (marijuana) bushes are difficult to spot from the air. They often look similar to other vegetation, and they are sometimes disguised between corn or other crops. Heavily-armed drug armies protect the plantations and the farmers who work in them. Soldiers going into these situations prepare for vicious fighting. Some local people welcome the raids. They make money by rebuilding the factories and airstrips, earning $10 per day!

◁ In 1986, the United States sent 160 soldiers and 6 Black Hawk helicopters to assist the Bolivian army in the battle against cocaine growing and drug production.

△ Annaberg Airstrip, a staging post for private flights transporting drugs, is almost hidden in the jungle of Manang Province in Papua New Guinea.

▷ Up in smoke: a drug trafficking airstrip in Colombia, 1988. But the strips are quickly repaired by local workers.

In Pakistan, soldiers destroyed 41 heroin factories in a recent year – with little apparent effect on production. In 1988 in Colombia, almost 90 tons of cocaine were seized, and 900 laboratories and 76 airstrips destroyed. Yet the cocaine supply to the United States appeared to increase after this effort.

Soldiers, specialists and advisors from the West are often sent in as part of the international drug campaign. The American armed forces and Drug Enforcement Administration (DEA) play a large part in the efforts to stop drug production in South America. Thirty DEA agents were sent to help the Peruvian army in the remote coca-growing areas. President Bush has instigated a five-year aid program for Colombia. Britain has recently given $1,600,000 to Bolivia to cushion the impact of the loss of drug crops.

The lords fight back

△ Victim of narcoterrorism: the work of the *Sendero Luminoso* of Peru. Such killings act as a powerful warning to those who try to infiltrate and expose the drug business.

The money made from drug trafficking is guarded by the cartels and the organized crime rings that depend upon it. Their ruthlessness, and the wealth at stake, mean there are no limits to the violence. There is a long list of officials, particularly judges and politicians from South America, who have been recently assassinated. Rodrigo Lara Bonilla, the Colombian Justice Minister, was killed for an estimated sum of one million dollars in 1984. Senator Luis Carlos Galan of Colombia was murdered in 1989.

Evidence suggests that members of international terrorist groups sell their bombing skills to the drug cartels in return for money to buy weapons. This helps the drug business to dispose of money, and it also fuels the international trade in illegal arms and their shipments. It is very difficult to trace such funds.

In the front line
In 1986, President Victor Paz Estensorro of Bolivia asked for American military help against cocaine production. The drug lords responded by assassinating him. Many officials put their lives on the line in the war against drugs.

When terrorizing individuals does not work, drug cartels resort to mass terrorism. For the last ten years, plane hijackings and civilian bombings have been associated with terrorist organizations such as the Irish Republican Army (IRA), the Palestine Liberation Organization (PLO), and Basque Separatists. But today there is a new term for drug-linked terrorist attacks on innocent people: narcoterrorism. In 1989, 111 people were killed when a plane taking off from Medellín airport was blown up — presumably in an operation organized by the Medellín drug cartel.

It seems likely that many terrorist organizations in troubled lands such as Afghanistan, Iraq and Lebanon are at least partly funded by drug trading. In Northern Ireland, the Ulster Defense Regiment is alleged to have bought guns with drug profits.

△ In 1989, a bomb planted by the Medellín cartel blew up outside the DAS national security headquarters, Bogotá, Colombia. It killed 62 people, and many more were injured in the incident.

Partners in crime
There is evidence from the explosives used that the bombing of the offices of DAS, the Colombian security and intelligence headquarters in Bogotá, was perpetrated by ETA, the Basque separatist terrorist organization.

Secret cargoes

It is illegal to take drugs across most international boundaries. But the drug empires depend upon the transfer from producer to consumer for their profits. All manner of methods and people are involved in the smuggling, and the penalties for those who get caught are high. The drugs follow routes that are complex and constantly changing. The authorities have yet to follow a consignment all the way from its place of origin to the users.

Both planes and boats are used to carry drugs across the seas. Private planes convey only small loads over limited distances, and are more easily noticed. Ships can carry larger cargoes and anchor off remote shores, away from the eyes of customs officers. Smaller boats are then used to ferry the cargo ashore, in true smuggling fashion. Much of the cocaine now entering Europe via Spain and Portugal is landed in this way.

Bribery is also used in the smuggling process, to make customs officials, police, airline staff and port authority workers "look the other way."

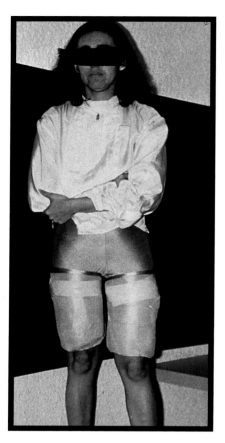

△ Courier caught at Miami Customs, 1989, with pouches of illegal drugs concealed beneath her clothing.

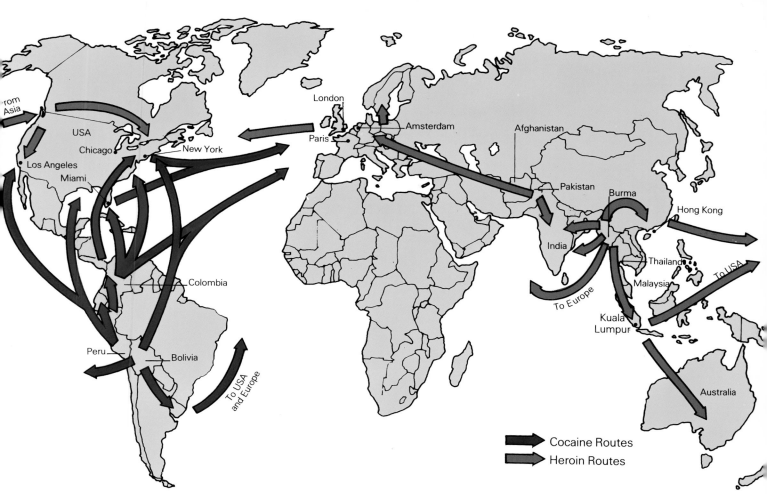

Cocaine Routes

Heroin Routes

△ Main smuggling routes for cocaine and heroin.

▽ Graph showing total numbers of domestic drug seizures in the United States in kilograms. Yearly increases probably reflect more drugs being smuggled.

year	1983	1984	1985	1986	1987
heroin	302	346	447	382	375
cocaine	7,399	11,742	18,129	26,954	37,148

◁ A haul of illegal drugs, disguised as imported confectionary, is discovered by customs officers. No consideration is given to children's lives put at risk.

In 1989 a 35-foot boat, the *Rough Diamond*, was used to smuggle $3 million of marijuana into Wales. Recently customs officers discovered a consignment of drugs hidden beneath the false floor of a container at the seaside resort of Felixstowe, England. The drugs were removed, but the container was allowed to continue its journey to the Midlands. In this way more of the drug smuggling gang were arrested.

Sons of a Brazilian judge, Osvaldo and Magnus Bernardi, were caught smuggling 13 kilos of cocaine into London.

Drugs are smuggled on commercial flights by couriers, concealed in their clothing and luggage, or even sealed in little packets and swallowed. This practice can go horribly wrong. If just one of the bags breaks, the courier suffers a massive overdose and dies.

Customs forces

Customs officers have the task of intercepting illegal goods coming into their country. Much of their budget is now directed at drug smuggling. About 95 percent of all drug seizures are made by customs. There are 900 preventative officers in Customs and Excise in Britain; in 1988 they seized drugs to the value of $200 million. These forces operate mainly at the airports and seaports. They work closely with police, coast guards and customs agents from other countries.

Customs officers have great power. They can search any person, package, luggage or vehicle which they suspect might contain illegal drugs. The use of sniffer dogs, trained to respond to the faint smells of drugs, has been very successful. So have spectrometer-type robot "sniffers" such as the CONDOR contraband detector. They are routinely used to monitor luggage as it comes off planes from drug-exporting areas.

Guardians of shores
In the United States there are thousands of miles of deserted coastline. The United States Coast Guard and Customs have a colossal task. More customs officers are recruited every year, and they develop increasingly sophisticated ways of detecting drugs.

▽ Miami maritime reconnaissance planes search coastal waters, while the surveillance helicopters track suspicious craft inshore. Boats and crews are searched when they dock. The United States Coast Guard now has over 40,000 staff.

△ Security staff from a major United States West Coast corporation stake out a probable drugs deal, using sophisticated remote-control microphones, cameras and communications equipment. Video cameras and microphones are frequently used by such security officers to provide recorded evidence for later use in court.

Target: Europe

The United States has long been the target of dealers in heroin, cocaine, and marijuana. The number of addicts in some areas seemed to be stabilizing at the end of the 1980s; possibly certain markets are becoming saturated. To preserve their trade and profits, the drug lords looked to a new market.

In 1988, Spanish narcotics detectives seized 1,000 kilos of heroin at Irún, in the Basque district. At the time, this was the biggest single drug seizure ever made in Europe.

Spain has since become the main route for drugs entering Europe, channeling about 40 percent of drugs heading for France, Britain, the Netherlands and other countries. Despite increased penalties for trafficking, there are now over 60,000 Spanish drug addicts.

It is clear that the drug lords have directed their efforts toward Western Europe. Interpol, the international law enforcement agency, estimated an increase of 350 percent in the amount of cocaine available in Europe between 1987 and 1988. This drug is worth almost three times as much in Europe as in the United States.

△ Lebanese farmers grow opium poppies in the Beka'a Valley. Heroin production here is controlled by various local militias, well armed and protected, as well as by organizations such as the Abu Nidal terrorist group.

22

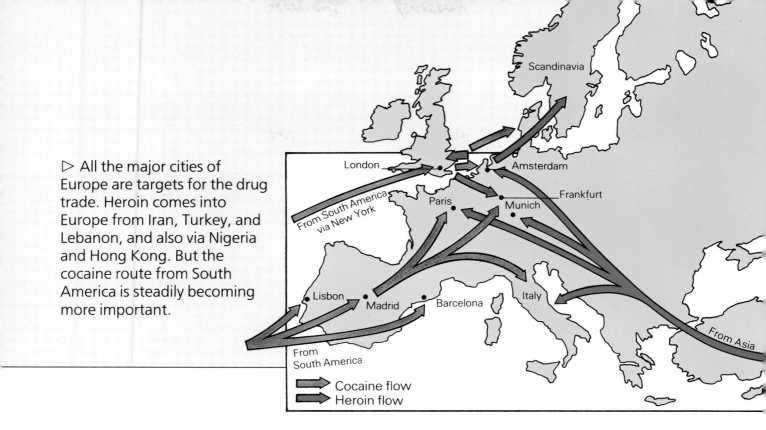

▷ All the major cities of Europe are targets for the drug trade. Heroin comes into Europe from Iran, Turkey, and Lebanon, and also via Nigeria and Hong Kong. But the cocaine route from South America is steadily becoming more important.

Scandinavia

London Amsterdam

Paris Frankfurt

From South America via New York Munich

Lisbon Madrid Barcelona Italy

From South America From Asia

Cocaine flow
Heroin flow

▽ Drug squad officers in Paris search for drugs. European cities are experiencing increased drug trading as some American markets seem to level off. Now even small towns have places where drugs are regularly offered for sale.

All European countries are reporting increased drug offenses. In 1986 in the Netherlands, heroin seizures rose by 66 percent on 1985; cocaine confiscations doubled. In West Germany, heroin abuse went up by 30 percent in 1987; cocaine abuse by 55 percent. Cocaine seizures have gone up in Britain from 85 kilos in 1985 to more than 400 kilos in 1989.

In Britain over 45,000 kilos of marijuana were seized in 1988, a seven-fold increase in ten years. Amphetamines and heroin are the most widely abused drugs in Britain. But the pattern is ominously changing as crack and cocaine become more available.

◁ David Medin, an American drug smuggler arrested for carrying cocaine in London, implicated the Irish Republican Army for arranging his trip to Glasgow, Scotland. Part of the profits generated would fund terrorist activities.

The chain to the buyer

All the way along the chain of drug production and distribution, criminals make money. The ones who lose are the addicts at the end of the line. The whole pyramid of drug trafficking and profits is financed by users, who may turn to dealing and become more deeply involved.

Cocaine and heroin leave their lands of origin already processed into fairly pure powder. They are usually smuggled this way because there is less bulk to carry for the value of the drug.

Drug wholesalers buy large quantities of drugs from smugglers and couriers. They "cut" it, package it into smaller quantities, and sell it to dealers. The warehouses or premises where this is done may also be used for legitimate business. Dealers or pushers sell the drugs on the streets. They have a group of customers, some of whom may be addicts. There are no controls over the way drugs are "cut," and users have died from poisons included in the fillers.

▽ Drugs are usually imported in a fairly pure state. But at each stage of distribution the dealers increase profits by "cutting" the drug – mixing it with a filler, such as lactose, chalk, or talc.

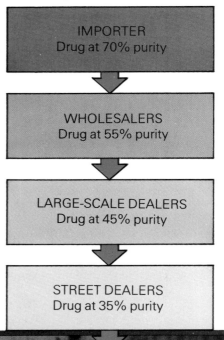

IMPORTER
Drug at 70% purity

WHOLESALERS
Drug at 55% purity

LARGE-SCALE DEALERS
Drug at 45% purity

STREET DEALERS
Drug at 35% purity

USERS
Pay $80-$400 per half ounce

▷ In Paris, like many other European cities, street deals occur openly in certain areas. The crime that goes along with drug addiction also takes place on the streets.

In some cities the violence linked with street corner dealing has become rife. Gangs shoot it out for control of an area's trade, and to protect their own incomes.

There is a network of communications so that the arrival of drug shipments can be advertised to the customers, who then raise money, ready to buy. When a drug wholesaler or dealer is caught and put in prison for a long sentence, his or her place is soon filled by another. There are many people already involved in the drug business, who have nothing to lose and money to gain, by moving into the lucrative vacancy.

Regular users and addicts must fund their habit. Often they have no job, and resort to theft or prostitution. One of the greatest problems of the drug war is that the trade is self-fueling. A relatively easy way for an addict to raise money is to start dealing in drugs as well, supplying new customers. These in turn become hooked. And so the net widens.

The violence associated with street deals has brought ordinary life to a standstill in some cities, where the residents are in fear of their lives.

Devising new drugs
The ideal drug for a producer is one which is easy to take and which is highly addictive. Crack is one example – when smoked, it has immediate effects and soon results in a craving for more.

▽ Acid House parties, a phenomenon of the late 1980s, involve inviting people from a large area, often in rural places. The venue is kept secret until the last moment, to prevent interference from the authorities. Drugs are usually available, and nontakers will be encouraged to try them.

Destroying the network

Success in the drug war depends largely on the ability of the policing forces to find and break the distribution networks. But the networks are cleverly designed so that no one person knows more than they need to. At each stage there may be several variables; a wholesaler, for instance, may have several "warehouses." Crack houses, where people go to smoke crack, are found in many large cities. They are heavily fortified – police have had to use oxyacetylene equipment and hydraulic rams to break into such places.

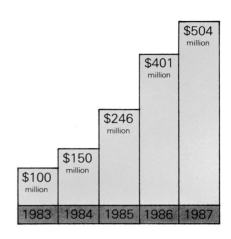

| $100 million | $150 million | $246 million | $401 million | $504 million |
| 1983 | 1984 | 1985 | 1986 | 1987 |

◁ Graph of assets seized from United States citizens between 1983 and 1987.

▽ Marshals of the United States Police Force in Washington raid a crack house in 1989. Such places are often well protected and guarded by armed criminals. By the time the police break in, the users have fled.

Police forces all over the world are being strengthened to cope with the increasing drug problem. In the United States, authorized phone taps and other "intercepts of communications" linked to drugs rose from 127 in 1970 to 379 in 1987. The New York police force recently created a 300-strong anticrack squad. In London the antidrug squad numbered 200 in 1987 and has since risen further.

These numbers are reflected by the increased numbers of drug-related arrests made by the authorities. Yet the amounts of drugs available and the numbers of addicts still rise. The justice and prison systems cannot cope with the numbers of criminals involved.

In the past, people who lived in areas where drug taking is common have been intimidated into keeping quiet about the problem. But lately, residents are beginning to react against drug deals and fights on every street corner. There are mounting civil campaigns to drive away dealers and addicts. This is another line of attack in the war against the drug trade.

△ A crack dealer is arrested in Miami. United States drug-related imprisonments rose from 1,945 in 1980 to 6,388 in 1987, the fastest-rising cause of imprisonment.

Can we win the war?

The drug war is being fought on various fronts. The countries where the drug plants grow are trying to rid themselves of corruption, replace the farmers' income with crops that do not involve drugs, destroy the factories, and root out the drug lords so that they can be brought to trial. But the large-scale dealers have seemingly unlimited funds and no inhibitions about using violence against innocent people. There is international aid, both financial and military. Customs officers and police all over the world seize drugs as they pass from country to country.

Those found dealing in drugs face heavy penalties whenever they are caught. Huge amounts of money are being spent on the war, and many people on both sides have died.

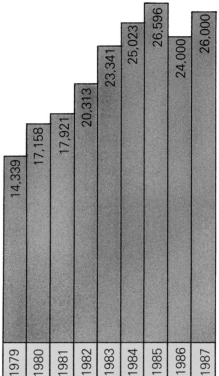

1979	1980	1981	1982	1983	1984	1985	1986	1987
14,339	17,158	17,921	20,313	23,341	25,023	26,596	24,000	26,000

◁ Drug related offenses in Britain increased steadily during the 1980s. Some experts believe that another wave of drug trading is ready to occur in the 1990s, centering on heroin. 1990 saw a record opium harvest in the Golden Triangle area.

▽ Confiscated drugs being burned under armed guard in Mexico, 1988. Some say that confiscated drugs should be sold to raise money for poor countries, such as Peru and Bolivia. Other experts disagree completely with this approach.

Some experts suggest that addiction should be treated as a social problem rather than a criminal one. They feel that efforts should be made to improve the lives of those likely to take drugs, so that they will not feel a need for them.

The ideals, however, are still to stop users taking drugs, to destroy the illegal drug networks, and to crack down on producers. In April 1990, a world ministerial drugs summit took place in Westminster, London. Representatives from more than 100 nations met to discuss how to tackle the world drug crisis.

In the same month President George Bush ordered the crack US "Green Berets" to Peru, as part of a $35 million package to help train and equip the Peruvian army in their drug war.

△ Virgilio Barco, President of Colombia, has led a determined effort to destroy the drug cartels despite violence and death threats.

△ In 1989 Monica de Greiff, who had become a symbol of Colombia's fight against the drug lords, resigned as Minister of Justice.

29

Hard facts

One way to ease the drug problem is through education. Rather than shrouding drugs in mystery, and letting their effects be subjected to imagination and false approval, the hard facts about their dangers are being widely publicized. People in possession of the facts about drugs and their effects will be in a better position to make up their own minds.

Teachers and parents are also encouraged to find out about drugs and drug abuse, so that they can recognize when young people are in danger, and learn how to help.

Drug Helplines

National Institute on Drug Abuse
Treatment Referral
1 (800) 622-H-E-L-P
This hotline is staffed from 9.00am to 3.00am on weekdays and from 12 noon to 3.00am on weekends. Counselors can talk with you, refer you to a drug treatment program, or answer questions about drugs, treatment, health or legal problems.

New York State Division of Substance Abuse Services
1 (800) 522 5353
This toll-free number reaches counselors who can provide referrals for treatment or legal advice, or over-the-telephone crisis intervention.

Heroin
Other names: Big H, Scat, Chi, Junk, Smack.
Origin: Produced by chemical processing of the opium poppy, grown in many tropical and subtropical regions.
Appearance: A white or dirty-white powder, or in tablet form.
Method of taking: Injected just under the skin or into a vein. Can be smoked in a cigarette or heated on tinfoil and the fumes inhaled ("chasing the dragon"). Also may be sniffed (snorting).
Effects: Euphoria, dulled pain and senses.
Risks: Users may suffer addiction and consequent withdrawal symptoms, overdose, poisoning from impurities used to "cut" the drug, infections carried within the bloodstream such as hepatitis and AIDS if injected, and death.

Cocaine and Crack
Other names: Coke, Flake, Snow, White Lady.
Origin: Produced by chemical processing of the leaves of the coca plant. This is grown in South America, Taiwan, Java, India, Africa. Crack is produced by heating cocaine with chemicals.
Appearance: A white crystalline powder. Crack is small, pale, opaque rocks.
Method of taking: Cocaine is taken by snorting or sniffing into the nose, using a tube-shaped implement; it can also be injected. Crack is usually smoked.
Effects: Euphoria followed by anxiety and hallucinations.
Risks: Convulsions, violent behavior, psychological dependence, overdose, death. Crack is highly addictive.

LSD
Other names: Acid, Flash, Tab, Paper mushrooms.
Origin: Lysergic acid diethylamide is synthetically made in chemical laboratories, mainly in Europe and in the United States. Hallucinogenic drugs also exist naturally in certain types of "magic mushrooms."
Appearance: A colorless, odorless, tasteless liquid, that can be absorbed onto any substance — blotting paper, sugar lumps or tablets.
Type of drug: hallucinogen.
Method of taking: Usually taken by mouth.
Effects: Unpredictable even to experienced drug users, usually altered perceptions and hallucinations.
Risks: Violent behavior due to a "bad trip," depression, flashbacks.

Amphetamines
Other names: Speed, A, Ups, Pep pills, Christmas trees, Fets, Co-pilots.
Origin: Synthetically manufactured anywhere with a suitable laboratory and chemical supply, mainly in Europe and the United States.
Appearance: Looks like a coarse off-white powder, or various kinds of tablets.
Method of taking: Swallowing, snorting, injection, or sniffing.
Effects: Amphetamines are known as stimulants and their effects on an individual are variable. Symptoms may include aggressive or energetic behavior followed by tiredness and depression.
Risks: Psychological dependence, infections carried in the bloodstream if injected, overdose, hallucinations, convulsions, and even mental illness.

Marijuana (Cannabis)
Other names for the various form: Dope, Ganja, Hashish, Hash, Grass, Pot, Weed, Bhang.
Origin: The cannabis plant grows in Africa, Asia, North and South America, the Caribbean.
Appearance: Herbal cannabis or marijuana looks like tobacco. The resin or hash is a resinous slab. Cannabis oil looks like black treacle.
Type of drug: Hallucinogen, relaxant.
Method of taking: Smoked in "joints" or "reefers," or mixed into cakes which are eaten.
Effects: Induces relaxation, elation, intoxication. The drug combines the effects of a relaxant and an intoxicant, not unlike alcohol in some respects.
Risks: Hangover, lethargy, depression, and lung cancer if smoked.

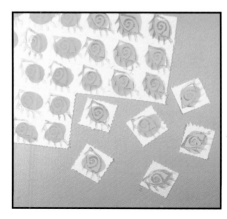
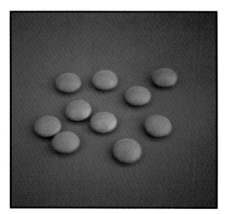

Index

Photographic Credits
Cover and pages 8 right, 15, 16, 18 top, 20-21, 22, 22-23, 24, 26 and 28: Frank Spooner Agency; page 4-5: S. Mieselas/Magnum; pages 6-7 and 14-15: Robert Harding Library; pages 6, 8 left, 9, 10, 11 top and 25: Topham Picture Library; pages 7, 12 all, 17, 18 bottom, 23 and 29 both: Rex Features; page 11 bottom: David Browne; pages 14 and back cover: F. Scieanna/Magnum; pages 21 and 27: Magnum; pages 30 and 31: Roger Vlitos.